Also by Edwin Morgan from Carcanet

Collected Poems
Collected Translations
Selected Poems
Sweeping Out the Dark

EDWIN MORGAN

Virtual and Other Realities

CARCANET

First published in 1997 by
Carcanet Press Limited
4th Floor, Conavon Court
12-16 Blackfriars Street
Manchester M3 5BQ

A CIP catalogue record for this book
is available from the British Library
ISBN 1 85754 347 5

The publisher acknowledges financial assistance
from the Arts Council of England

Set in 10pt Palatino by Bryan Williamson, Frome
Printed and bound in England by SRP Ltd, Exeter

For birth but wakes the universal mind
Whose mighty streams might else in silence flow
Through the vast world, to individual sense
Of outward shows, whose unexperienced shape
New modes of passion to its frame may lend;
Life is its state of action, and the store
Of all events is aggregated there
That variegate the eternal universe.

(Shelley)

De innumerabilibus immenso et infigurabili;
seu de universo et mundis
        (title of book by Giordano Bruno, 1591)

Acknowledgements

Acknowledgements are due to the following, where some of these poems have previously been published: *Verse, London Review of Books, Honest Ulsterman, Cencrastus, Parataxis, Object Permanence, New Statesman and Nation, The Dark Horse, Ibid, Cutting Edge, Times Literary Supplement, Cambridge Journal of Comparative Criticism, New Orleans Journal, Private Arts, Skinklin Star, Salt, The Big Issue, Southfields, Orbis, Poetry Review, Oxford Poetry Quarterly, New Scottish Writing.*

A Voyage was commissioned by the BBC and broadcast on Radio 4 on 12 June 1996. *Beasts of Scotland* was commissioned by the Glasgow International Jazz Festival and was set to music by Tommy Smith, first performed on 4 July 1996 (now on CD, Linn Records, Glasgow).

Contents

A VOYAGE

A Voyage

The Sperm

In the beginning the sense of being was dim.
I do remember the first body, the man's,
Where I was herded haplessly with so many others
Through gloomy twists and ducts, till suddenly
I felt my own movement – like being born, that was –
As unseen vessels poured their milky fluid
Over us, and we swam for dear life –
Yes it was life, must have been – down
At first, then up that unforgettable tunnel
So narrow we were panting against one another,
Pushed onward, truly propelled, as long pulsations,
Shuddering contractions and expansions – what power! –
Shook the tunnel wall and drove us jostling
Into what I thought would be upper air.
How wrong I was! The explosion was volcanic,
The release, the scattering, the four, five waves
Were like the climax of some giant act
We were and were not part of. It had put us
In another place, another body, another tunnel
Enormous after the one we left, alien,
Acid, terrifying, formidable, wonderful!
What a sight we were! Imagine first
A revolution in some city square,
A million people gathered swarming, gesturing,
And then imagine four hundred such cities,
Drag them together like images on a screen
And watch the seething, struggling mass. Can you?
Can you count four hundred million souls? 'Souls'
May be pushing it, but you know what I mean –
The word slipped out, I'll let it stand. Well then,
We were there, in the woman, *in vivo*, in her caves
And galleries and underground streams, an army
Of explorers, aspirers, tunnellers, Galahads,
The living, the sick, the dying, and the dead.
You maybe think one sperm is like another,
But oh, not so, I can tell you. Acrobats,

13

Loonies, power rangers, Columbuses, moribunds –
I saw them all. In that first scatter-shot
They spread in such a monstrous tangled blash
Some never could swim free. I watched a trio
Twined together, sinking. There was a tailless one
Feebly shaking its head. One swam backwards.
Some wriggled or darted aimlessly. One broke in two.
Pieces and runts were scavenged by prowling cells.
Tidal waves swept millions out of sight,
Down, down and out, I've no idea where!
So life is tough, I thought, but on we go.

I swam strongly, up into the tunnel,
Learning that movement, quite as much as force,
Was what mattered. The head, like a snake's wedge,
Must weave from side to side, the tail must thrash
With rhythm, the whole body must trace
The five points of a star. As I looked around
Through the thinning millions, I was well out
In the vanguard, and cut quite a dash
(If you will forgive me) with my tail's
Obedient and flexible fibres, the fructifying bands
Of power-pack energy at my midriff, and oh
The treasure of the three-and-twenty threads
That throb, none broken, all perfect, in my head,
My hungry prow high-pointed towards the Other,
Which I shall find. Am I too confident?
I do not think so, though I know my rivals
Whom I see coming and going, never far
From the front, recognizable – did you know that? –
Some male, as I am, some female, I can tell them.
There's one I call Michelangelo, a bruiser
And no mistake, thickset, dour, powerful,
Swims in quick bursts, shaking head like a dog,
And dogged he is, I must watch him well.
His opposite is elegant to the last degree,
Thin, sleek, cutting ravishing curves
With her tail like a hair from the bath: I call her
Nefertiti, and she almost smiles.
Then there's Bonnie Prince Charlie, flighty
And slight, yet with an unmistakable flair

As he flirts his short tail like a kilt and steers
An unsteady but undaunted upward course.
My favourite, though, is one who might win home
Against the odds: she's hard as nails, she swims
Angular, awkward-seeming but not really so,
Her fibres and articulations shine
As she shoulders (you would *think* she had shoulders)
The seminal webs apart; I fear and like her,
She's my Sigourney Weaver. When I say 'like',
What do I mean? Could two sperms fall in love?
I am given to speculate, but there's no *time*.

I'm off. Cells are flying, waters weltering,
Strong contractions in the tunnel wall
Draw me along till I'm more boat than swimmer.
But that's too good to last. A sticky curtain
Guards the narrower paths and conduits ahead,
The caves and shafts and desperate isthmuses
We have to squeeze through, shedding companions
By the hundred thousand at each station.
Well, that gloopy mucous mass is push
And push and push again, with a special thrash
Of the tail and a mighty thrust and we are through.
I am through, that's the point! It is my story.
Poor Charlie slipped, what frantic pirouettes,
But then he lost all sense of orienteering,
Diminished, vanished down the lurid adits.
Onward the rest, potholers at the vestibule
Of caverns maybe measureless to man
But not to us! Into the penetralia!

The Egg

Waiting, waiting, silent and still,
What I must fulfil, I will.
I rolled, I lolled, I oscillated
Along paths anciently created.
I'd love to say that I 'broke free'
From the sac that constricted me,
But no, I was expelled from it,

And though I knew I had the wit
To say 'I am', I only moved
When fleshy fingers had approved
Of me and pulled me in, and tunnels
Drummed me wetly forward, funnels
With bristles tickled me like a trout,
Dandled me about and about,
Fondled me into this resting-place
Where I can rock, and dream, and face
The butting heads and lashing tails.
What does nothing, yet prevails?
That's me, that's my magnetic power.
But times there are, in darker hour,
The prison of my sphere assails me,
And something like a teardrop veils me.
Oh to be truly free! but I
Must wait like an unsleeping eye.

The Sperm

The caves are full of – what are they full of? – us,
Sliding waters, pulsing walls, wandering cells
But not the right one yet. How strange to think
This mechanism, this place with all its splendours
Interlocking, planned, crafted, long perfected,
Should be a cradle of adventitiousness
At our level, a rough chaos of sloughed
Cellular stuff and smurf, earthquakes of posture,
Din of irregular waters, fragments of things
You could not give a name to, an environment
That would faze all but the most intrepid:
Keep Piranesi, wipe the Taj Mahal!
The smaller you are, the more you see of its workings.
Not that I see myself as small at all.
I deduce it from the majesty of the voyage.
Well, it prepares us for the world outside!
Contingency keeps order on its toes.
I love it. I'm not complaining. My strokes
Are strong, in rivers murky or clear, I jostle

The debris as it judders past, I gauge
The turns and angles like a skater.
                              Nefertiti
Is weakening, in her exhaustion her slow tail
Wags like a run-down clock, she's falling back
In a fading flaunt of beauty, a last tilt
Of that chiselled head. She's only one of many.
Where are the millions? Tight junctions loom
For a struggling hundred or two, a caravan
Of battered, flagging desperadoes kept going
By tinglings, breathings, scents and apprehensions
– Impossible, but there it is – of goals,
Ends, embraces, giving and taking of treasures –
They feel it, I feel it – let us press forward,
Brothers, sisters –

The Egg

Not a wish, not a notion.
There really is a dim commotion
Quite near the cave. Is my waiting over?
Where is my sailor, where is my rover?
Nothing is easy: worst and best
Are still to come. Can you invest
My fort? You want drawbridge, doors,
You must try elsewhere. No floors,
Roofs, bells, stairs? What will you do?
I am not here to frighten you.
Well yes I am! but that's the way
To pull the hero into play.
Very slowly I am revolved
As if my host had now resolved
To show me to the Argonauts
Alive, complete, and theirs. My thoughts
Are on another life to come,
Grown like a bramble, not a plum.
The walls tremble. Wash through then,
Nature, joy of gods and men!

17

The Sperm

                              This is the chamber.
Something must happen. I was weary, but not now.
How many are left, a dozen? Cavernous is the word,
With many things dark, or stirring, half shining,
Shapes even here, though it is far more tranquil
Than the first tunnel, that seem made to disconcert.
What are those cells, lookalike bodyguards
For the one cell we want? And sperms like ghosts
From some earlier encounter, what are they doing
Still knocking at the door? Why don't they die?
And all those stains and trails, milky graffiti,
MENE MENE TEKEL UPHARSIN of the underworld,
Are they a warning, a welcome, a nothing?
                                        I swim
With broad strokes, further in, wondering.
Suddenly it is there, it, slowly turning,
The thing, the egg. My god but it is big,
More massive than I had ever imagined.
We circle it warily, as if it might bite.
But it is closed, baffling, aloof, impregnable –
At that joke I snapped out of it, looked hard
Across its surface, watched my companions,
Began to manoeuvre. I am not the first.
Michelangelo has breenged forward like a bull –
Finesse is not his forte – stubbed his blunt head
On the unyielding egg, broken his neck.
His body pieces twist down out of sight.
After so many adventures, it is grim
To see the death of the strong. Strength will not do,
I thought, or will not do enough. Surely
Sigourney would know, she would not fail.
Ah, but a fold in the cave wall released
A vicious alien, a sperm not one of ours,
Stringy with jealousy and disappointment,
Who fastens onto her and twines about her,
Dragging her struggles off into the dark.
Sigourney, Sigourney! I would have cried out,
But she is gone. Apart from a few stragglers
I am alone. What am I here for then?

Our host, this monstrous hustling watery dynamo,
Has purposes beyond our knowledge, not
Beyond our wonder, which is an early kind
Of love. Who would not tremble as that egg
Trembles? She guards it, yet she wants it entered.
I have to re-enact the very deed
That gave me life, I have to penetrate
The very flesh that drew me in before.
I swim up close, my head buzzes, ferments –

The Egg

Now I feel a clear vibration,
And I tremble with elation.
What use is solitariness,
Mother only of distress?
I slid and surfed into this place,
Washing my daunting carapace
With waters that protect and feed
And keep alive the primal need.
Whoever knocks at my doorless shell,
Be bold, be hard, be sweet, be fell!
Nothing less mixed will force me to
Open my brooding heart to you.

The Sperm

Close up, it's almost too big to be seen.
You have to fight your way through a waving wood
Of filaments, a crown of thorns, a cumulation
Of cellular fuzz and fuss, a *noli-me-tangere*
If ever there was one, but so what?
It whispers as you wade in. You don't believe
A word of it, and push. At last you see
The surface, the zone, shining, tough, pellucid.
You gather your energy, your head throbs,
And head body and tail flail in a frenzy
As you attack the sphere. God, I am there,
I am fixed, I am sprawled, I am crucified
Like a living fossil: can't stay like this!
How to get in? I never felt my jaws
– Jaws? why not? – so powerful, they eat,

19

They cut, they gnaw, they dissolve – revolve –
It's like a drill of enzymes – what an idea –
But it's oblique, more like a camel-bite –
A lively, deadly slit – you can almost hear
The zone sighing as you wriggle through –
Sinking into the universe of the egg.
I knew there would be change, but not this change.
My tail has lost its force, oh, all its service;
It snaps, it is gone, somewhere into the smush.
My body is crumbling, going, it is broken
As I am broken in this grainy blinding egg-white.
Its power-pack seems to have migrated
To my head, my beautiful jewelled snake's-head
Which grows and grows until it almost bursts
But doesn't yet, everything is fine, we lose
To gain. How do I know? I am slowly drifting
Towards the goal, the throbbing tingling packet
Of secrets, the egg within the egg, the twin
I have at last myself become an egg for,
To meet with till the two are one again.

The Egg

Now you have no escape from me,
But I have ways to set you free.
Your three-and-twenty treasures lie
Swimming in a last joy with my
Three-and-twenty treasures, and
This is how we grow a hand,
Get a foot to walk the sand.
It is a grace to understand.

The Sperm

My three-and-twenty treasures I freely give you.

The Egg

Our six-and-forty treasures will outlive you.

Sperm and Egg in Unison

May nothing ever, then or now, misgive you.

BEASTS OF SCOTLAND

Wolf

Bring back the wolf!
He's not long gone, you know.
He went out when sheep came in.
Sheep cleared men and women.
Now let wolves clear sheep.
A little wildness please,
a little howling to be heard from the chalets,
a circling of yellow eyes at Aviemore.
That legend much discredited,
of the following of the sledges,
let us test it in the Cairngorms,
in the winter playgrounds with their merry cries,
in the white paths through the forest.
It would be good to get not a few scalps
to crawl with fear when they hear
that eerie arctic song
as one by one the muzzles
lift and open in the dark,
and the dark is long.

Golden Eagle

Soaring, soaring,
dancing in the heights of the air,
swooping to slice each other's flight-paths,
two courting eagles
display their dark desirability
over the frozen boulder-fields.
It is not cold to them up there.
Their instincts burn them through the winter sky
like meteors. They do not call or cry.
Their blood is a song to them
as they quarter the blue that is not for prey
but for love, and the dim thought
of more eagles.
The white hare
goes about his business in a snow-drifted corrie
where the shadow of those huge wings
is for once as harmless as a cloud.
Soon some claws will come down on his back
when the hungry mate is on her nest,
but not today,
not now,
while the winged things are tumbling in their delight.

Red Deer

We are the deer
and we are here.
We like it here.
We couple and we fight,
eat everything in sight,
and some say that's not right.
We're nearly half a million strong:
suppose we ran in unison,
gliding like a spreading stain
across the windy high terrain,
who could cull us, who could kill us,
smell of stalkers couldn't chill us.
– That's a dream we sometimes dream
beside the falls and roaring stream,
and then we wake to rifle-cracks
and feel the kitchen at our backs.
Brothers, get those antlers clashing!
Bellow if the rain is lashing!
Sisters, trot through bog and heather,
take dainty fill of every weather!
Ears cocked, nostrils flared,
browse and watch, don't be scared.
Watch and browse, green delight,
shoots and roots, soon comes night,
soon comes snow
when you must go
starving and gaunt
downhill to haunt
the homes of men.
What then, what then?

Midge

The evening is perfect, my sisters.
The loch lies silent, the air is still.
The sun's last rays linger over the water
and there is a faint smirr, almost a smudge
of summer rain. Sisters, I smell supper,
and what is more perfect than supper?
It is emerging from the wood,
in twos and threes, a dozen in all,
making such a chatter and a clatter
as it reaches the rocky shore,
admiring the arrangements of the light.
See the innocents, my sisters,
the clumsy ones, the laughing ones,
the rolled-up sleeves and the flapping shorts,
there is even a kilt (god of the midges,
you are good to us!) So gather your forces,
leave your tree-trunks, forsake the rushes,
fly up from the sour brown mosses
to the sweet flesh of face and forearm.
Think of your eggs. What does the egg need?
Blood, and blood. Blood is what the egg needs.
Our men have done their bit, they've gone,
it was all they were good for, poor dears. Now
it is up to us. The egg is quietly screaming
for supper, blood, supper, blood, supper!
Attack, my little Draculas, my Amazons!
Look at those flailing arms and stamping feet.
They're running, swatting, swearing, oh they're hopeless.
Keep at them, ladies. This is a feast.
This is a midsummer night's dream.
Soon we shall all lie down filled and rich,
and lay, and lay, and lay, and lay, and lay.

Conger Eel

Down, down, diver, drift into darkness,
down among the rocks, down among the wrecks,
cling to your lifeline, let your knife shine,
watch for the big one, something is stirring,
sniffing for its victim, something is shifting,
sifting the sand, peering from portholes,
barely breathing at the barnacled cabins –
shoots out, lunges for a luckless lobster,
snaps, crunches, threshes, head-shakes,
gulps, crunches some more, ripples,
dances – can you see it, diver? –
three metres of muscle, scaleless and sleek,
dancing in its palace of anchors and deadlights –
what a sway, what a weave, what a yaw – but watch it
conger! and watch it diver! – watch out! –
they're caught in a tangle of fishing-lines,
they fight the lines, they fight each other,
it is the diver's undreamed-of nightmare,
dragged and wrapped up by a conger,
a couple thrashing the silt in nylon
like sado-masochistic lovers –
the knife, he still has it! – hack, missed,
hack again, slice, tug, rip through
the lines, they fall, he's disentangled,
kicks up and off to his own world.
The conger trailing broken nets
plugs his angry foundered hold,
and the dead ship is his once more.

Gannet

High the cliffs, and
blue the sky, and
mad the spray, and
bright the sun, and
deep as the grave
the teeming waters
never at rest
in St Kilda's cauldron.
Fish for the taking
lazing in innocence
island to island,
flesh for a thunderbolt
not thrown by gods,
not a Greek, not a Gael.
If the fish could look up:
a bird left the crag
white against the blue,
half hovered, half circled,
stopped in an air-path
with eye unblinking,
folded its wings, and
gravity-batteried,
sharp beak down, and
sharp tail up, it
plunged, it
plummeted, it
hit the sea, it
shot right under, and
vanished except
to the fish it speared
in a fearful irruption
from a heaven unseen.
So who is safe?
The gannet cliffs
are shrieking, but
not about that.

Spider

Bruce lay on Rathlin Island
Listening to the rain.
The dreary skies weighed heavy.
Would he go home again?

'Why do I skulk on Rathlin,
Hiding in caves and barns?
What use are drag-tail exiles,
Polishing rusty arms?

The wind buffets the boulders.
The shower stalks the sea.
The grass waves back and forward.
All this is nothing to me.'

Bruce gazed up at the rafters
From his pallet of prickly straw.
He moved his flickering candle
To be sure of what he saw.

In a corner of the roof-beams
A spider began to swing.
It measured up the distance
But the thread refused to cling.

Six times the spider dangled
With the mocking web half-done,
But the seventh time was perfect,
The persistent heart had won.

Said Bruce, 'I love this creature,
I'm schooled, I'm dared, I'm told
To kick my own six failures
Behind me, and be bold.

A seventh time for Scotland:
The sword, the sail, the oar:
Baptize the flag of freedom
With blood on Carrick shore.

It's not too late, my fighters.
My friends, it's not too late.
Like patient, steady spiders
Construct the Scottish State.'

Seal

– Mother, I can hear a baby crying,
Out there in the sea, is it drowning or dying?

– No no, my lamb, that's not what you hear.
It is only a seal, go to sleep, never fear.

– There's another, and another, oh it is so sad.
How can an animal make us feel bad?

– I don't know, my dear, maybe they smell
The fishermen with clubs, fearful and fell.

–Why do they kill them? No wonder they cry.
Do the men never have a tear in their eye?

– Oh no, the seals kill the beautiful fish
That make our supper a beautiful dish.

– And we kill the fish. Everything we kill.
We dig a grave and it's too big to fill!

– Darling, it has to be. We are killed too.
Seventy years and the message comes through.

– Oh mother, the night is so cold and so wild!
Listen, listen, I am sure it is a child!

Wildcat

When did you last see me?
Never, perhaps.
You saw the ferns moving – was it the wind?
It's true the fronds are a good camouflage
for my stripes, but I can tell you
I was not there, not then.
Does that make it any easier,
I mean, that you really failed to miss anything?
If you still want to meet
this shy, solitary, rare etcetera –
well do you? – one of those days
when I am not snatching rabbits
but casing your chicken-coop? –
not extinct, you know, maybe a spirit –
spirit of Scotland, eh? – I haven't lost
my drift: here you are then,
meeting me, at the wire of the hen-run,
twilight woods behind, I'm doing my crouching
and spitting, gently lashing a bushy tail,
all right? You want to communicate?
Try to stroke me, lose a finger.
Try to tame me, lose a face.
But frankly this is academic.
I shun farms, crofts, dogs, guns; I've had that.
Where I love to be, I doubt
if you will ever find me.
I prowl the high bracken.
I am comforted by the rocks.
I rub the harsh trunks
of the Caledonian forest,
a ghost among ghosts.

Salmon

We hung over the falls, watching.
The river groaned as the gorge narrowed,
its turmoil was white, extravagant.
All this was far below. Once through,
it was crashed on by the waterfall
in a sort of massed chaos. The splashes
were brilliant, the spray was very fine.
A rainbow dared to cross the uproar.
That was not what we came to see.
But there they were, one, two, six,
some red, hook-jawed, stacked and packed with
energies they brought from Greenland,
backs, snouts testing the spumy
half-air half-water element
they must jump through, even fly through –
they sprang, they soared, they gaped, they gasped,
lashed frantic tails, fell back, quivered,
lurched up again, making it, some,
some stunned on rocks, but a great one
first, high, and his mate soon after,
nonchalant, nudging each other over
the sexy gravel of the spawning-beds,
the cock and the hen, in their last fettle,
ecstasy of the cloud of eggs,
ecstasy of the burst of milt,
the thrust of indomitable life.

THE FIVE-POINTED STAR

Catherine the Great

He sounds like just the man. I'll have him here.
His genius deserves a wider sphere.
I wrote to Voltaire, why not try for Burns?
He'll serve me, yes he will, he'll serve my turns!
What could he miss? He'll be at home with us.
Cold blasts? An unmistakable plus.
Strong drink? We'll toast him under the table.
Superstitions? We've reams of myth and fable.
They say he's rather hard on royalty.
Well well, but that was France, we'll see, we'll see.
In any case, I want to pick his brains
On profitable subjects, crops and drains,
To take steps to improve the steppes (I must
Stop this word-play) which are more *thrang* with dust
Than waving stalks (yes, I've been reading Scotch),
Scotch stalks, ha ha, I really ought to watch
This tongue of mine, it must be the new year
Or the full moon or getting into gear
To send a letter to Caledonia.
I don't need either onions or ammonia
To get my eyes to glisten when I think
Of Rob – I know he isn't Rabbie – and clink
My bracelets and my ambers and twitch my gown
And scratch an impatient pen and throw it down
And pick it up again and make myself proper
To write a dignified yet piquant offer.

(What I did not say was how we'd take a sleigh,
The two of us, one tingling frosty day,
With trusty driver, trusty horse, and skim
The wolfish forest paths, I'd sing to him,
He'd sing to me, we'd both be wrapped in sable,
Wishing the swishing tracks interminable.
And if his hand should creep into my muff,
That would be nice, that would be nice enough.
I did not say that there are joys and joys.
You get so tired of raw-boned stable-boys,

37

A jump, a thrust, a grunt, and *do svidaniya*.
I'd rather sleep with Anna or with Tanya!
I'm only joking. But a clean and witty farmer
Might be my last and unresisted charmer.
All this I did not write, but he can read
Between the lines, for his need is my need.)

James Macfarlan

'A man's a man for a' that' – how does *he* know?
Traipsing with his plough, the rural hero,
Swaggering down the lea-rigs, talking to mice,
Sweating his sickly verses to entice
Lassies he'd never see again, strutting
Through the salons in his best breeches, rutting
In a cloud of claret, buttonholing
Lord This, sweet-talking Doctor That, bowling
His wit down levees, bosoms, siller quaichs –
D'ye think he's ever heard the groans and skraighs
Of city gutters, or marked the shapes that wrap
Fog and smoke about them as if they could hap
Homelessness or keep hunger at bay? What,
Not heard or seen, but has he even thought
How some, and many, and more than many, survive,
Or don't survive, on factory floors, or thrive
Or fail to thrive by foundry fires, or try
To find the words – sparks scatter and bolts fly –
That's feeble – to show the new age its dark face?
The Carron Ironworks – how he laughed at the place,
Made a joke of our misery, passed on
To window-scratch his diamond trivia, and swan
Through country-house and customs-post, servile
To the very gods from which he ought to resile!
'Liberty's a glorious feast,' you said.
Is that right? Wouldn't the poor rather have bread?
Burns man, I'm hard on you, I'm sorry for it.
Your flame dazzled, folk gave you glory for it.
I think such glory is dangerous, that's all.
Poetry must pierce the filthy wall
With cries that die on country ways. The glow
Of bonhomie will not let the future grow.

Sir James Murray

I pick a daimen icker from the thrave
And chew it thoughtfully. I must be brave
And fight for this. My English colleagues frown
But words come skelpin rank and file, and down
They go, the kittle kimmers, they're well caught
And I won't give them up. Who would have thought
A gleg and gangrel Scot like me should barge,
Or rather breenge, like a kelpie at large
In the Cherwell, upon the very palladium
Of anglophilia? My sleekit radium
Is smuggled through the fluttering slips. My shed,
My outhouse with its thousand-plus well-fed
Pigeon-holes, has a northern exposure. Doon
Gaed stumpie in the ink all afternoon,
As Burns and I refreshed the dictionar
With cantrips from his dancing Carrick star!
O lovely words and lovely man! We'll caw
Before us yowes tae knowes; we'll shaw the braw
Auld baudrons by the ingle; we'll comb
Quotations to bring the wild whaup safely home.
Origin obscure? Origin uncertain? Origin unknown?
I love those eldritch pliskies that are thrown
At us from a too playful past, a store
Of splore we should never be blate to semaphore!
Oxford! here is a silent collieshangie
To spike your index-cards and keep them tangy.
Some, though not I, will jib at houghmagandy:
We'll maybe not get that past Mrs Grundy.
– But evening comes. To work, to work! To words!
The bats are turning into bauckie-birds.
The light in my scriptorium flickers gamely.
Pioneers must never labour tamely.
We steam along, we crawl, we pause, we hurtle,
And stir this English porridge with a spurtle.

Franz Kafka

Poetry, I think, is but a minor art.
In this dark life of ours the hardest part
's to make ends meet and not go mad. He knows
Better than most, this Burns, this exciseman, he chose
The business, he fed his family, he manipulated
The system with some success, some panic. He rated
A 'does pretty well for a poet' in the records,
Was due promotion when they dropped the cords
On his early coffin. What was the cost of this?
Patrons rise behind patrons, you hit, you miss,
You try again, grovelling's a groove of the time.
As for rivals, watch them watch you climb.
Who's a pretty boy republican?
Not me, I'm royal blue, I'll kiss the crown.
How well I know his guilt and fear! I see him
Riding eight hours a day, nothing can free him
From the dismal well-paid search of auld wives' barrels
To find among a wheen stowed cheese or farls
The beer, the brandy, the baccy, even the tea
He has to impound for half the goods and a fee.
He warned them sometimes, let them off. Was that good?
What is a good exciseman? How can he brood
Over the shillings in his ledger – the king's
Shilling! – when heads are rolling and rings
Are cut from the half-dead on battlefields?
Battlefields? Nearer home nothing yields
To pity. My last client lost his arm
On the shop floor. Everyone knows the harm
Was 'accidental', management was clean.
No one's going to subpoena a machine.
How could I stretch the wretched compensation?
His empty sleeve mocked my deliberation.
We're both bookkeepers, Burns, so what adds up?
Who kicks the bucket and who wins the cup?
Did you do your best after all? Did I?
You were a fighter with a melting eye,
And what more can be honoured? You had reach –
'I am going to smash that shite Creech!' –

But the blue devils could penetrate your shell
And dance the black exciseman off to hell
If you let them. You didn't. I don't. I think I don't.
How can we live with only use and wont?

An Anonymous Singer of the 21st Century

It's all on CD-ROM. Look under Song.
It's hyperpackaged and you can't go wrong.
It's under Scotland too, and Education.
Burns holds up his umbrella for the nation.
Possess this sangschaw and you'll think no book
Need burden your shelves. Click, listen, look.
The text of every song is there, the notes
Of every setting, sounds from the blended throats
Of the best singers made electronically one.
Every place referred to is flashed or run:
Here you have Afton Water, Ailsa Craig,
The Pier o Leith, Largo, and Stirling Brig.
See Auchterairder! See Parnassus Hill!
Abraham's Bosom! Take a pill, make a will.
And press the translation service, do not miss:
Drive the ewes to the hillocks. One affectionate kiss
And then we separate. Of all the directions the wind
Can come from. O what happiness I gained
Fixing new teeth in a comb for dividing flax.
– But what of the man himself, you ask? What tracks
In the snow, what drawing-rooms, horses, shebeens?
No actors melodramatize those screens.
Digitized Burns is mixed from every portrait,
Strides like life across the fields, goes straight
To his chair, frowns, hums, fidgets, sings.
Remember his 'rich, deep' voice? It rings
Through the room, his eye smoulders the wallpaper.
Is this, you think, at last, the mover and shaper,
The makar and not the Mandelbrot? It's not.
Its strange perfection disinherits thought.
Switch on a hundred times, you'll learn no more
Than what was doled out at the cold blank door.

The real songs linger at a fugitive table,
Amazing, changing, bold, supreme, able
To get the hardest eye to glisten, heart
To throb, vessels of a profuse art.

I sing to please myself now, or for friends.
Great songs may have uncovenanted ends.
The stream of love, hope, memory, incitation
's too naked for this packaged generation.
But hear me if you will, and then you'll take
A joyful draught with me for that man's sake.

Note: James Macfarlan, Glasgow working-class poet (1832-1862).
Sir James Murray, born Roxburghshire, editor of the
New English Dictionary (now the *Oxford English
Dictionary*) (1837-1915).

44

VIRTUAL AND OTHER REALITIES

March

A wilder March I never saw for sleet.
I feed my fax, and watch the whitening street.
I send the southern sun sheet after sheet.

The signals go, the page remains, the snow
the hail the ice dissolve, the driven show
shouts like a flare before it's forced below.

Our pounded earth stokes and stews and seeds.
Every invisible shape salts its needs.
What's unknown splits and re-splits, drinks, bastes, breeds.

The crocus-perky hail-beds don't feel brave
or anything so human, but they save
a certain braveness in us, to give the grave

a kick or two from legs still there. The fax
is in the land of numbers, covers its tracks,
its impulses like rations brought in packs

across a thousand miles can only say
the dialling hand is up and on its way,
braced by one raffish, restless, rude spring day.

The Ferry

The ferry shudders, chugs, noses, quests.
A sailboard like an angel skims the crests.
The land of rhyme is active: nothing rests.

The farther shore, the darker blue, the smudge.
Get to the bow, get your binoculars, budge!
It's a long island, but you have to judge –

watch! – your landing on a place so virtual
its blue might be a blues, a throb, a spiritual,
it searching you, you it, mute, mutual.

Never believe it! – buffet, buck, breach
dimensions like meniscuses, give speech,
cry out, scrunch your keel right up the beach.

The sailboard like an angel-fish head on
has virtually vanished, only to don
a shimmer that long after it has gone

you could stand watching, waiting for the time
when it must turn and be itself, and chime
with what you know is real on waves of rhyme.

Mare Firmum

'Walking on water wasn't built in a day.'
No, but watch for signals through the spray.
Bear with the endless beckoning of the bay.

Gigantic water-boatmen moonbeam zigzags
get your feet itching as you're sucked from moss-hags
by power of salt, wind, cries from skuas' crags

out into the element where if you run very fast
– think of ashy fire-walkers – you'll soon have passed
the hurdle of fear; or let yourself be cast

like a stone to skim the welter – can a man
not beat a stupid stone – what is the ocean
but testing-ground for slingshots, rataplan!

Practical plodders will make shoes like boats,
lean forward, lift and flop their crazy floats,
shout to each other from a team of throats –

but theirs is not the meaning of the game.
Only the naked foot must make its name.
Perhaps by fasting, a light and airy frame

might with a frail shirt for a sail be blown
across the choppy tops, a saint alone,
till faint and fading he is the sea's own.

At last it seems nothing will do. You sit
on the machair, the dawn mist lifts a bit
as you stare at imagined figures threading it.

They seem so calm, to minds on shore, that few
could guess the wilds of will they've long come through
to tell us we must sometime walk there too.

Into Silence

They are all gone into the world of sound!
There is no cutting-room floor, no ground.
I speak, and I am nowhere to be found.

Words lap then zap the circuit; pungent air
burns the benches bare, spectators spare.
The late boom of a poem raises hair

but cannot stop to wrestle silence. Voids
must be bursting like silos. Steroids
cannot be pumped into odes – or odoids.

If we could map that land, we'd surely go:
to *Penny Lane*, to *Visitatio
Sepulchri*, to *Green grow the rashes O.*

We'd still be running there, all ears, intent
to know what happens to the joy that's spent,
the stanza's end, the loan that won't relent.

I think it would be good to hear that place.
The finished tape would not re-trace but trace
its noble scroll in one untampered space.

Threes

Pythagoreans love to take their ease
in a clear calm country rich in threes,
breakfast with trivet billies on their knees,

pant under triliths as the midday heat
curls their pumpernickel and they eat,
drink, snore, twitch where dolmen shadows meet;

but at day's end they wake, to rise and welt
the starry hunter's triple-worlded belt,
stretch, and try on the vision of his pelt.

In the Kitchen

'A bunch of asparagus in a teapot'
comes at us, not quite part of the plot
but life all the same, more so as it's not

clichéd geraniums or a small cute cat
with its tail in the spout, enough of that;
no, it's the sturdy meaningful straight-bat

incongruity of that crock of tendertops.
What hand stuffed them, laughed, said 'Pour the crops!'
She doesn't spend all morning in the shops.

I love that imagined briskness and quick striding
into a room, the tilt of head, the deciding
never not to risk a prim deriding.

Nothing surreal; no pot on the rooftop,
no bride in the sky with crowns of greens to drop.
You cannot say I want the world to stop.

But I'll buy order with a pinch of salt.
I'll bless the windfall of a sprightly fault.
I love the *sdvig* that tells the pomp to halt.

The Heart of Midlothian

He's killed his father, don't know it yet but will.
Red hands grip crusts till he has scoffed his fill.
The tight cords hurt his body – not his will.

Bandit, savage, reiver, devil, scum –
he's saddled with his titles till kingdom come.
To him, useless resentment's long gone numb.

His eyes pierce through his own darkness; his skin
is windburnt, dirtpocked; black hair thick, face thin,
his frame all sinew and hunger. Lose or win,

his sixteen years are ready as a fox
to twist and run; he's been sold like a box
of tools and will be again; money talks.

He's unbaptized and nameless; likes that well.
'Call me the Whistler,' he says, 'I'll go to hell
in my own way, eat the fruit, eat the shell!'

He's killed his master on the dire plantation,
indentured into brutal detestation,
unholdable in any servile station.

He's in a tepee now, his logs are sawn.
He mimics the wild beaks and wings of dawn,
an undrawn life worth more than all the drawn.

1818

Despite his manacles, the wiry murderer
in the death cell broke a bottle of porter,
slashed his throat, but death was out of order –

blood-red Matthew was patched up by his jailer,
made half decent for the hanging, all the better for
white cap, white gloves, tied feet and hands, miner

with no dirt on him, Matthew Clydesdale, actor
to a massed milling of hard starers, leaper
out of this world, carted in coffin of fir

with his death in order, under halberds as was proper,
up the Saltmarket in a dreary November,
into the College, to the anatomy hall where

Matthew must act again. The professor-dissector
gowns himself in white, bows to the theatre
of buzzing tiers, introduces an experimenter.

A Glasgow Frankenstein is Doctor Ure.
The hanged man sits unbound in an armchair.
His dreadful face faces the handsome professor,

the avantgarde chemist, the galvanic battery. Air
enters his lungs, his tongue wags, eyes flutter,
limbs convulse, he stands, amazed, aware –

his death is not in order! In the uproar
shouts, faintings, shrieks, applause conspire
to let Professor Jeffrey lance the jugular

with theatrical flourish. At his third death, the collier
leaving the electric arms of his resurrector
slumps in the blade-cold arms of his dissector.

Clear the hall. Pity the executioner,
pity the murderer, pity the professor,
pity the doctor with his battery and his ardour.

Under the Helmet

I watched a camel saunter through the eye
of a needle and become a cable. I
saw two broad-winged pigs taxi and fly.

Quart pots settled nicely in pint jars.
Bright gondoliers poled the canals of Mars.
Sailors were sipping tea in dockside bars.

With one bound Jack was free with one bound Jack
was free. This is the front that has no back.
The jacket is first black, then white, then black.

Strap in. Begin as stick and end as drum.
Freewill's predestination's kingdom's come.
Press the sensor to its maximum –

you've crossed the road. The traffic and the day
are brillianter than paradise, though grey.
You laugh, and throw the dizzy gear away.

Someone will pick it up to range again
through all the worlds imagination's men
loom up with like old Grendel in his fen.

Brisk Thoughts towards Town

What was that thunder that kept drumming off in droves?
Who keyed those searings blasting green from groves?
Why were there blights that blue-bloomed hour-old loaves?

Rhetoric, like colour, melts off the edge.
We never jumped from the blue window-ledge.
We never jumped. We were picking at our kedg-

eree and had toast popping, napkins, best tea
there ever was, a light rain out, the sea
beyond the second field, and our well loved tree

which was only an old rowan dripping down.
Breakfast so early it seemed the very crown
of dawn munched us with brisk thoughts towards town

and what the hell was virtual reality
to smacked lips, fingered chair-backs, individuality
of crumb, fishbone, pleat, fork, a sodality

stung into life by sunlight on the knife:
the run of things as grateful to be rife
as ever mouse and cursor were. A fife

throbs to be shrill, but cannot, in its case
by the door. We dust the case, replace it, pace
behind pace, heartbeats not virtual, face behind face.

A Dream Recalled

They soaked his black tobacco in poteen
and let him chew himself into a dream
where nothing was but only seemed pure green.

The sky was like a billiard-table there.
Gingerhead boys had emeralded their hair.
Sheets and shrouds dripped up from kelpen lair.

Green was the laburnum in the sun.
Green was the sun, green the unburning one
the moon, in starfields of viridian.

The old man grew more restless by the hour,
as chewing jaws and juices lost their power.
He glared at last at true grass like a giaour.

Shamrocks, good god! They'd left him by the hedge.
But he had been far out, over the edge.
He hated the stiff windless ranks of sedge

that were only themselves, as he must learn to be.
His chuckling mates brought leprechauns to see
their work, and to extort a fitting fee.

'Chew the quid, and spit, and scratch your arse.
You'll never get to Venus or to Mars.
To be a good bit player in a farce

you must forget the transformation-scene.
Bluebells are blue and bowling-greens are green.
And leprechauns are seldom to be seen.'

The man cried out that he would never rest
until he saw that green light in the west:
the red sun may be good, but it is best!

More Questions than Answers

'Can acupuncture cure pins and needles?'
Can bumbledom regalvanize the beadles?
Can the fed hand bite back what it wheedles?

Improbabilities are *de rigueur*.
Hearts are primed to heat-seek, *alles Natur*.
Pass me the ashen light, *por favor*.

You make the story as you go you make
the story even if you go you take
the story on the go and watch it break.

So far this poem does not have a focus.
The wandering locum cannot keep his locus.
Lit, sweet, hand-rolled, we're passed to friends to smoke us.

The curtains nearly meet, the iron steams.
Reality, though straining at the seams,
may still press on, hunched there in the moonbeams.

All right that's it. Make a kirk or a mill o't.
You are not like to find nothing of note.
Buy a season and don't miss the boat.

North to the Future

NORTH TO THE FUTURE – Alaska's number-plates
have no truck with those unsophisticates
whose space and time are separable states.

Hurry, snocat of the steely slither!
Take us where ice-flowers never wither.
Pluck us through the tundra like a zither.

Twentieth-century Anchorage twinkles blank.
The twenty-first dawns glamorously dank
on Baffin's foggy walrus-haunted bank.

The twenty-second is a prickly hush.
Prospectors pause. Dogs whine in vain to mush.
The stars of Labrador rise up and rush

towards an undetermined destination.
Hear that high shriek of ice, like indignation!
Spitzbergen's turbines moan in desolation.

On – on – never dare to stop!
Powers take blips, but time's an endless crop.
Fusion frigates lash the polar top

till waters well and spin their blooms. Who
can catch the thirtieth as it races through,
faster as furthest ages always do?

Centuries near the speed of light are sledged.
Centuries past the speed of light are pledged.
For unimagined keels keep whale-roads dredged!

The World of Things Undone

Want something done you must do it, do it.
A never to pain and you'll always rue it.
It comes back, it chokes, it corrodes, eschew it!

The world of things undone has far more matter
than this one, its vaults and vats far fatter,
its deep-groyned orange sands too dense to scatter.

The castles you can build, and drinks to drink,
pack that space to which you have no link.
You hesitated at the cloudy brink.

Tables are laid there, not with food that kills.
The food that kills already steams and swills
in pretty clingfilm from your bursting tills.

It's ordinary, it's great, we can't not take it.
How can we think of heaven, and then make it?
This is our thirst, not that, it's easy, slake it.

And so they sit back filled with nothing, staring
at shadows, fit for a yawn, abruptly glaring
if you say bearing nothing is not worth bearing.

Keep the door shut, it's a dark wind out there!
I can hear dragons scratching in their lair!
– Get out, you fools, and breathe the dragon's air.

The Fourth World

In the fourth world, you can sometimes hear singing.
The rain is sullen and the mud is clinging.
Stumps are weeping, sodden rags are stinging.

Where there were buildings there had then been huts.
Where there were huts, a few slashed water-butts
are left to drink aready poisoned cuts.

Rubbish is swirling in chaotic gusts,
bones, bullets, cans, bag-ends, fag-ends, crusts.
Legs fight the innocently vicious thrusts.

At night, with bark and cough, beast after beast
gnaws into arms too weak to fend the feast.
Red eyes fade, lope off at the red east.

Daybreak bloodies a foundered caryatid
that shoulders only dust; ants make a bid
for cracks, people for graves; their hopes are hid

so that it seems impossible one so old
stands up and flaps a shawl into the cold
in order to make sure that the untold

stories are told, and still there in her singing
the world she knows outlasts its perilous bringing
to shimmer like a whole bell ringing and ringing.

The Poet

'And leave him simply the great true recorder',
not seeking order, or the measured disorder
of chaos theory, but pressing every border,

scouring, tracing, probing and extending
whatever tries to tell him it's an ending,
breaking whatever tells him it's unbending.

Leave him to count the bodies in the city.
His clothes hang dusty and his hands are gritty.
Leave him to fumble to a well, for pity

it seems only the water-drops can proffer
when human gun, torch, mine, shell, hatred offer
nothing but clapped-out coffin, cleared-out coffer.

Leave him to walk the roads of wars, grudging
no bloodied yard as he pants forward, trudging
with refugees in the high passes. Judging

but silent, he takes paper, writes. Booty
litters forgotten paths, dogs sniff. His duty
struggles to keep at least an iron beauty.

Words, bitter as tears, are overflowing.
Words better than tears are doggedly hoeing
fields that seem past harvesting or sowing.

What poor great creature then? He limps, he prowls,
winces when something deep inside him howls.
His line reminds, entices, soars, grieves, growls.

The Glass

To love you in shadow as in the light
is light itself. In subterranean night
you sow the fields with fireflies of delight.

Lanarkshire holds you, under its grim grass.
But I hold what you were, like a bright glass
I carry brimming through the darkening pass.

The Dead

It is not true to say they are not here,
the dead. Never gone but never clear,
they punctuate the room, the street, so near

you see the eyes set deep in others' faces,
some gesture that hooks out buried embraces
of how long back: other places, other cases.

Although they are silent we know we walk with them.
There needs to be no sorry stratagem
of note or phone, wave, grin, kiss, shout, tugged hem

to feel the virtue of the undenying presence
going out and out, spreading like an essence
that fills and spills and falls and never lessens.

How can living shapes be so invaded?
The unpersuaded cannot be dissuaded –
as if the red of dead leaves never faded!

It fades, yes it goes white and skeletal
until at last there is no leaf at all,
a vein or two, a mulch, a pith, a scrawl

like this on paper which remembers it.
I ask you who are dead if it takes grit
to people shadows when the lamps are lit

in Glasgow of this old world you once knew,
or if whatever has been loved comes through
if those who want it to are still and true.

The Pen

Thirty-four chips of mirror-glass are set
in the four sides of my ballpoint from Tibet.
My face is caught in them like fish in a net,

flashing in twisting facets as I write.
The handmade lozenges are rough, though bright.
So many pieces of me! I must hold tight.

I'm holding fast to everlasting snows,
to yaks, tea-bricks, choughs, mandalas, crows.
The frozen fall ecstatically flows.

It's all in this red far-brought throwaway
which as I use it drains off day by day.
What will the inkless shell be able to say?

'Roll me down the chute to the bin men.
One picks me up, tries me, useless, and then
it's truck of teeth, grindings, bits of pen:

Orpheus was no better. My diamonds gleam
through the dread dead, the garbage, the black scream.
Make me your crunch, your glitter and your theme.'

The Race

Crowding out east into the North Sea roar
white canvas whips and flashes and gulls soar.
Two million watchers line the dark Tyne shore.

Blowing off to Bergen like a blossom that has burst
from its harbour mast-forest, the tall ships thirst
to be free, to be thrust, to be trusty, to be first.

A hundred shining square-riggers white with boys
have pushed the cheering shoreline back; a noise
of ropes, commands and sea-slaps rounds the buoys.

The slap of water and the creak of wood
are powers that the crowd has understood.
Ancient with sails, the day is wild and good.

Yet the tea-clipper run is dead and gone.
The young men heave and climb for dreams. A dawn
from the crow's-nest is fine – painted or drawn.

Two million people must be real; the keels
are really in the water; who conceals
the unreality the ocean feels?

No one. For here the virtual and the real
are married, and such human scenes reveal
our longing for the plenum of the weal.

Early Days

'The growth of what is excellent is slow.'
Still in its womb, the universe we know
waits to come out. A simple scan will show

the pack of cells, the pulse, the push, the stir,
the creeping and the creaking and the whir,
the absence of a titan accoucheur

not even yet on call. Such early days,
inchoate centuries! Millennial rays
very gently warm the hedgeless maze:

the maze, the plot, the net, the knot, the heart,
the tuft, the beat, the loom, the thrust, the start,
the grit, the silt, the salt, the shine, the chart,

the swirl, the sift, the two, the break, the three,
the surge, the drive, the five, the fire, the scree,
the gush, the crash, the roar, the gush, the sea,

the air and the eleven and the cloud,
the lung, the luck, the thirteen and the crowd,
the seventeen, the shrivelling of the shroud,

the tugging of the cord, but not in panic,
the peals, the nineteen, throbbing but not manic:
until the prime cry tears out, weak, titanic.

Universes

'No one knows our universe is unique.'
Flype it, and be prepared to hear it speak
in tongues, vibrations rising, fading, weak,

not to be understood. Its doubles, brothers,
sisters, shadows: how much more those others
must breathe in secret, unimaginable mothers

dead and preserved, packed in Plutonian cold.
And some are scarcely born, and some so old
no time exists for their story to be told.

No time exists at all for some: pure space
compacts them like a nugget of pure grace,
you sniff them hot, each one a grain of mace.

But cry for those that are all time: unseen
impalpable unclosed they drift and glean
nothing but what interminably might have been.

Image and no-image interlock
in poetry. It is of ancient stock.
Night and day the universes dock.

And day and night the gantries slip from sight,
the horn is heard that puts our doubts to flight,
the word moves out with casings clean and tight.

The Tomb

'We have this task here and we have no other,
to lift out quickly cleanly our red brother,
and bury him at last beside his mother.'

'He is not here. We opened all the tomb
to make such preparation. Yon chill room
lay empty, the glassed place had some faint bloom.'

'Where were there guards? Were no guards got that night?
Not a moon too. Did no one think that right
to keep some vigil, ears keen, rifle, light?'

'A blizzard must have bound all sentry blind.
Red granite took white shrouds as the wind whined.
Five letters, flaked, fluttered out of mind.'

'Well, shall we seek him, bratya, if far to go?
Must shall we run like wolves across the snow?
Thieves after thieves, to end such bitter blow?'

'The land is wide, or sea and sky, what then.
Yours is to go, ours is to watch again.
The stormy mother cries, but not amen.'

To the Librarians, H.W. and H.H.

Once I began casting my life away,
books and papers waved back quick to say,
New shelves, new selves! Far from the library

I shook myself like a wet dog and barked
through water-meadows, double-rainbow-arc'd,
splashes and sparkles lapped me where I larked –

a Pasternakian lightness, kicking the cumber
into others' vaults, levitating the lumber,
decimating the band but not the number –

until the hard white whistle of existence
halted me in my tracks with its insistence
on asking me if I felt no resistance

to peeling layer on layer like a flaying,
did I not hear the winds, the distant baying,
where was my life, what was Vesalius saying?

Why, there is no protection, I replied.
What you have been and done's not set aside.
Your files are you, and file through one divide.

Burn your letters, burn your boats: no tide
will ever wash away the ash you hide
of pain, or love, or pain or love denied.

The Burden

Whatever is a burden, let it go.
To tug and tie is futile, let it go.
Like Christian at the river, let it go.

Not that you'll muster with the winds, not that.
No one is unmelting trophies, not that.
It's not a one-off trebuchet, not that.

But oh you want to raise the dagged and drear ones.
You want to cut a clearing for the dear ones.
You want to hold and prop and urge the near ones.

Free as air and strong as iron, you'd do it.
Groans, guilts, bent backs, stubbed toes will never do it.
You know what you must loose and lose, so do it.

So do it and take heart, the roads are long.
Stride straight until the clean shadows are long.
Sleep an unburdened sleep when nights are long.

Dialogue

'You feel that you are feeling. You are not.
The kissing lips are red, but not red-hot.
The thrust that drains you must have cost a lot –

in softwear but not sweat. Weird when wired,
your passions never wilt, cannot grow tired,
you pout at demons if demons are desired.

Your brains and not your veins are packed with junk.
You saw a Giacometti and breathed "Hunk!"
You stroked the bright green feathers of a skunk.'

'What if I did? What if I should? What gunk
has jammed your mind-set? Why are you still sunk
in snore country? What's in your stuffy trunk?

I know what's in your stuffy trunk: the past,
clutching its flypaper black with the vast
flypast of brilliant wings it brought down at last

by patient dumb obstruction. It won't do.
Pandora kicks. Doors bang. Winds rush through,
releasing and seeding feelings we never knew.'

Realism

Realism counts the cracks in flags,
pains its charcoal round the limbs of rags,
brushes a hand's back against money-bags

swung over pavements to the bank's blank van,
cuts the quick of fantasy, Snatch it, man,
hop in a taxi, two fingers, Cayman –

turns the corner quietly, turmoil unseen,
velleities of crime, a mind too green
to kick-start action from the dream machine,

goes home, fills a kettle, flicks the boil switch,
how to describe the seething water which
hisses till it pounds up loud and rich –

or how it twisters through the clouds of tea
in the warmed pot, wildly contained, set free
by the strainer, dark gold streaming cloudlessly –

how to say the cup is waiting there
but does not know it is, shining to share
a shining, bare as waiting lips are bare.

Imagination

Imagination, power high entire,
springs from the flagstone with a crack of fire.
The very grave of earth smokes with desire.

Shaft, scroll, banner, torch, with the arms of it –
limbs, weapons intertwined, the blazon lit
by lightning – squeeze up from the pavement pit

like genies and swell in a tower. Dark streets
tremble. The militant flamboyance meets
dusk, midnight, dawn, it's pillars, crowds, fleets

rising, leaning, scaring, beckoning, flying,
it soars above the pulling and the crying
but it has clothed itself in the undying

prow, it is the nose-cone of the race,
its comets are the tresses of a face
turned upward into the blue cruel space

where we must do what we imagine doing,
and what we've done is not matter for ruing
but mainspring for the unimagined ensuing.

In Night City

Gibson Gibson Gibson Gibson Gib-son!
Hullo therr, goany geez a bliddy crib, son.
Dinnae wahnt some eejit tae gie ye a chib, son.

Ur aw thae radgie nuts in Cybernippon
guys an dolls yer hauns kin get a grip on,
an if they're no, whit screens ur they a blip on?

Is it blid, is it juice, is it a chairge, ur they randy?
Is their denner pretend-sampura wi trash-shandy?
Whit d'ye mean ye're no sure. That's handy!

Mise à nu par ses célibataires,
même, la mariée, gless right doon the sterr,
gless in'r herr, she's crackt, you're crackt, ye're a perr.

Deid-nerve black-magic necro-nigro-neuro-
mancer, no a chancer ur ye? Euro-
phobe, Pacific Rimmer, Yakuza Bureau?

Ach well. Whitever ye ur, Ah'll see ye aroon.
Ah've gote ma ain prosthesis in this toon:
the toon. See thon? See power? Whit a stoon!

Really Red

I walked out once to find the really real,
from early morning into cochineal.
That first mistake still seems to have appeal.

The category-master never cracks
a whip, or sneers, or swears, or leads attacks
on honest seekers, or stuffs poets into sacks

together with their misplaced consequences.
No, he just stands there, foursquare in his senses,
with light blue eyes to break down your defences.

Oh but you must be strong then to outstare him!
Nothing more is needed than to dare him.
The only thing you cannot do is scare him

which you don't want to do! For those blue eyes –
to give them flecks or flickers would chastise
the grand opponent you materialize

whenever you arc. Outface him and he fades,
with dignity, at failing barricades,
saluting you as he rejoins the shades.

I entered cochineal at half past five.
The red was really lividly alive.
I halted, with my mind in overdrive.

Mile upon mile, dimension on dimension,
a crimson chaos panted for invention,
for love, for the impossible intention.

For Love

What is more real than love? Unseen, unheard,
not even mole-like, not implied or inferred,
not born, not shot, not listed, not interred:

what is less real? Did you see it go by,
on the motorway, across the bay, the sky?
And yet the loss of it has made you cry.

We search so blindly through the absences
that nothing could more captivate the senses
than apprehended, silent presences.

We move towards them, feel that they enfold us,
plead with them to really want to hold us.
They disengage; they had to; so they told us.

But patience told me love was no illusion.
To stop pushing; fate takes no collusion.
To be so unintent that the profusion

of possible joy was not imaginable.
Until I pulsed into your throat, until
you pulsed into my throat, we took our fill

of things more immaterial, not more true.
What is eight years if the warm flood comes through
to do at last what waiting could not do?

If lovers often dwindle into friends,
friends can become late lovers, make amends
for habit, live with beginnings and not ends.

Armies of time, once summoned, are soon massed.
We run to meet them, disappearing fast
into a future that soon too is past.

In the Stony Desert

Those who loiter benighted at Lop Nor
soon find out what a caravan is for,
when spectral voices rise from dune and tor.

The solitary horseman starts, grows pale.
His name is called, he shakes, his spirits fail.
Good Marco Polo tells this not tall tale.

Friendly-frightening, knowledgeable, intimate,
the unseen speakers fade, return, debate.
Sands whisper, harnesses reverberate

in stillness and in cold. He hears the strings
of half-known instruments, and moonrise brings
drum-rolls, a summons, whinnyings, clashings:

where is that wandering steel, whose are the cries?
But footfalls leave no footprints for his eyes.
The djinn laugh softly, don't materialize.

He sweats, swears, shouts, gallops half-possessed
until he sees the lighted tents at rest
as if only order and peace were manifest.

A Mongol Saying

'All music is really about horses.'
Saddle and grass unite their swaying forces.
The pounded ground's sung through by watercourses.

Without saddles, even boys are centaurs,
father and brother black-browed bareback mentors
who've been with the wind and back in whooped adventures

to hoof a shed horseshoe from some dead horde
golden or black, too dull to be restored
but shining inwardly like the great lord

Jenghiz, the unforgotten. In his stirrups he rises,
his helmet points, his eye pierces, he advises.
Westward the unimaginable prizes

mingle with real mirages, whinnies, snorts,
dust-clouds of embassies from shaking courts,
letters of submission from rich forts.

Too much pawing and stamping. Off, away!
He gestures, and a pipe shrills into play,
another, and another, till the day

cracks like a sheet of overheated metal,
hundreds of high-pitched horses in full fettle
are nudged by naked knees to show their mettle,

and now the ten drums, tight-stretched, have begun,
and soon the thundering hooves and drums are one.
It is the music of the grass and sun.

Nightmare

Waking to crumpled sheets, an ancient fear,
my nightmare of three, four times a year,
I am lost once again, and day is not near.

Images of endless repetition,
yet never quite the same, haunt my mission,
which I can't know; to kill the inanition

I leave my room, the house, the street, I walk
through that large half-known town whose constant talk
twitters its unknown tongue; block after block

I try to saunter, but as day grows late
I panic, I am lost, landmarks disintegrate,
I have no way back, everything's desperate:

language, money, documents all gone:
I seem to be in rough fields, running on,
searching for my town which the horizon

keeps pushing further off, I'm on my own
in a scrubland of many roads, I groan
that every road is wrong, oh I've long known! –

at last there is nowhere to go, but run
I must, into the dark, all goals undone,
I must break through that darkness, three, two, one –

At the Last

My mother's last words as she fell, 'Don't leave me!'
have come back many times to re-bereave me:
I did not leave her, but they sear, believe me.

Hospitals and hospices are there to
soften the desperations we are heir to.
Hate death, fear death? That's something we don't care to!

But sometimes what they say can't mollify us.
The great dread is still ready to defy us
if we should think to slip out drugged or pious.

Slip out we may, but dark and solitary,
however many friends are watching; ferry,
pole, black water at the bedhead: wary

be, wary be! To hold a hand, to squeeze it
until it is so cold you must release it,
may be for the holder's pain, to ease it.

Hope against dread; the breaker breaks the bay.
I think of Everyman in the old play.
Only Good-Deeds would go with him on the way.

The Brink

Freesia, freesia, what a sweet faint scent
I breathe across the room, my head half-bent
over the table I write at, the daylight went

an hour ago, a lamp in the half-light
gleams on my mother's vase. I know the night
won't wait, must come, but I'll sit on in sight

of darkness and the window-pane, I'll think
of times – oh, at the very crumbling brink
where memories abseil a trustless link

across a gulf, a freezing, a crunch of fears
that not the flowers of a hundred years
could put to rest when that fresh scent appears.

Not that Scene

Trolling at St Vincent Street again –
only beware the rents and take the men –
after, tell me a little – how or when –

we've nothing hidden now, I know, you know –
hunger and desire, the raw and hurried blow-
job in the lane – the sporty car slung low

crawling, circling, jump in, judge a face
but don't go home, dark car park's the place,
slide the recliner for the interlace –

wrestling then for what you need, my dear,
my love, as I sit writing, burning here
listening to traffic in my midnight fear

your streetwise instinct failed you in some field,
back court, waste lot, canal bank, the congealed
haft of a nightmare with no cry, no shield –

oh not that scene; only a story to tell
we'd laugh at easily, of how you – well,
you pulled the string – like that – his joggers fell.

Indefinables

'A thought articulated is a lie.'
The threadworm challenged lobsters prancing by.
The lobsters thought the worm wobbly and sly.

A stately scuttle may seem contradictory,
but that's how plated jointed thoughts get victory,
kicking all wispy things their valedictory.

Articulated, hence articulate?
Thoughts in grammar picking out the state?
Thoughts in metre sent at highest rate?

'I don't quite really – do they? – sorry – think it –
if that's what – it's a voice you know – or link it –
broken – some lightness has a – plates could sink it –'

'Ah well, the threadworm had a restless night.
It can't stand undertow. We were all right.
We found some pots that hold us neat and tight.'

The world's half water, swimming like an eye.
Minds rest no more than seas, though they may try.
And then the sky. The sky. The sky. The sky.

On the Level

Some Language Poets gathered on the levee
to watch the sunset, with a quiet bevvy.
The usual low slaughter was red heavy.

Quite white water purple, what a trace
bandage buildings, mirror, the slapped face
hard shine, hand over the carapace.

A mill swim sounder, that if any, bounding.
An arm case dark, lung, infill, ironfounding.
An all there was, reflex, prey to surrounding.

Half diving strips. And even open wide,
opened, red cavalry sea well astride
a swell, shouts, footbrake this, that side.

Sink of ink where else but up, oh deadly.
Amber ember, win a lyric, redly
into walking over, stick a medley –

as if a Mississippi knew blue, note,
ingot, puddle, plumb down, the whole float
gagging, thrapple, craig, hass, last boat.

Bivouac pegging. Language licked a fight.
They were over the taken. Blood filthy bright.
Find a pressure point, run out of sight.

Zaum

'Ule Elye Lel Li Onye Kon Si An.'
When virtual poetry joins the caravan,
not what it cannot, please, but what it can

is your criterion for its board and keep,
undemanding as a nightingale, its peep
and trill and murmur breaking solid sleep

to dreams of mapless and unvisited
lemurlands – what, ring-tails in the bed,
I'd rather play some Messiaen instead –

no you don't understand, the human tongue
has shot into the mind, its prey is stung,
stunned, swallowed, it is not something sung

but something said when all is said and done,
watch the chameleon smack its lips in the sun
as its throat flutters and the juices run –

but what is substance if you can't define it,
what crude subsistence and you can't refine it,
what sustenance that cracks as you design it? –

I tell you its very duty is to be strange,
it hits you and you don't know half its range,
it leaves you with a world to rearrange.

And no it's not encrypted, for its plan
is to keep virtual. Concur. Don't ban
Ule Elye Lel Li Onye Kon Si An.

Someone

I just want to gather you to my –
jacket, breast, what is it? – I'm not high! –
but I can't bear to see you passing by

from there to here to there, unknown till now
and unseen ever after, it's not how
it happens I want to know, but what to vow –

libation, sacrifice, a week of time, a hand! –
to get you to come back and – I don't know – and
simply stand there? that hair, those eyes? Grand

it would be to have even that, for otherwise
you are not quite real, and again otherwise
you might not let me – and once more otherwise

I'd have to dig for you so dogged-deep
in thickets and mud of words I'd at last reap
nothing, nothing but a poem to gather and keep.

Marlowe

'In one corner lay his eyes, in another his teeth.'
Hurry to hell if you can with his wreath.
The floorboards are sound, he is not underneath.

All they that love not tobacco and boys –
God, what was that appalling wall of noise –
it's blotting what I thought were endless joys –

a scrunching and a wrenching, oh like nothing
outside torture-chambers, one scream cutting
the pig-throat night, high, long, followed by something

silence could only squirm to wash its hands of,
and legend, retching, try to make demands of –
plop of a roughly torn-out eye with strands of

nerve still clinging, then its neighbour, and the dice
of a few flung rattling teeth, the very paradise
of seeing and saying left there for rats and mice.

What happened to all those angels then?
What are they for, have they no care for men?
They drift off one by one, amen, amen!

O Faust, Johannes, broken, spirited out
into your terror, I'll write you and I'll shout
your godless power until it comes about.

Real Times

'I never had much luck on the rent scene –
got robbed at GHQ, boy of sixteen
with a blade – I was young then, and green –

Later of course there was the Old Quebec,
the only place where you could hit the deck
with forty-year-old rent boys, each a wreck

as well preserved as art could make him: I thought
not really, no, you'd have to want it a lot
– I did too – but getting it unbought

's as possible as always, exchange of fluid
behind the trees, come on you woody druid,
green but not green, into the dark, just do it!

It's not quite tirra lirra by the river
but then who wants the crazy threads to sever –
remember it a while, but not for ever.'

Giordano Bruno

Innumerable worlds and worlds unmade,
half-made, the universe immense, displayed,
half-hidden, hidden, infinite, arrayed

with lights or lying back in hungry black
till knots unknot and darkest packs unpack
and pouring creatures run through every crack:

oh yes they do! why should we think it dead,
that vast ubiquitous flicker overhead?
The staff of life may not be only bread!

Why would the lord of life confine his writ
to this one ball of water, flesh, and grit?
You say it's special? Ah but transcending it

are specks we see, and specks we cannot see
but must imagine, in that immensity.
It is reason sets imagination free.

Configurations still unfigurable,
visions and visitations still invisible,
powers to come, still impermissible –

these give the slip to my incarceration.
Chains and a cell are but one suffering station.
Multiple worlds need multiple incarnation.

– But earthly powers were called for, and were shown.
There is a sequence when the torch is thrown:
smoke, screams, a little ash and bone.

The Saluki

If all phenomenal objects are bundles of qualia,
how come we want to distinguish, *inter alia*,
the glints and scents from the realia?

A glance is not a facet but it needs one.
A facet's not a crystal but it feeds one.
A crystal's not a blizzard but it speeds one.

The blizzard's qualia are roaring cold
and choking white and fleeces in the fold
and some wild telling that is never told

because it will not stay for you to hold it,
no one has ever priced or poached or sold it;
slap days and nights of clay, you'll never mould it.

So it's not it but them, or those, or there?
Some hate what isn't solid, listed, square,
can't stand that wind in the saluki's hair –

but what does the Arabian hound dog care –
it runs with flounces in the welcoming air –
a hunter unbundling qualia everywhere –

can you run with it, not rest when nothing's at rest,
can you make a bundle of bees and swarm with the best,
can you set with the shifting carmines of the west?

Marginalization

'We have increasingly become phantoms.'
You can almost see our starving atoms.
We flit from Areopagus to Patmos

to Jupiter to Hell and any place
where we might find the remnants of the race
we're severed from, but there is no trace.

We pass through bastions, dungeons, pyramids.
Nothing stirs in the stone. Our heavy lids
drowse on the grilles and tills and screens and bids

of an unclassic time. Everything stirs
but falls again like dust, a soot of futures.
Dismay and deprivation hug the stairs.

Phantoms pushing nothing across counters,
phantoms in malls, a maze of non-encounters,
phantoms clocked by cameras and bouncers –

a blur, a shadow, something grey, half seen,
things to think back to, never really been,
an unclicked turnstile – the undead, the unclean!

Who has not felt this, as Gramsci once,
hammered by forces hard as distant suns,
made thirsty for a spring that dries, not runs?

Within the walls he writes most steadily,
encourages his friends, freely, readily,
heads letters with hope, and not wrong-headedly.

In a Bar

Bona homie, bona partso, hey?
Don't wind him up though, or he'll never play.
Leather gods can be a leery lay.

Did I ever tell you – oh it's not fair,
see the policeman's helmet, no underwear,
keeps shifting leg to leg, look, don't *stare!* –

I never told you about my leatherman,
turned out to be a rubberman, oh *man*,
got out a huge rubber bag, I almost *ran*,

put me in it and brought me off, drew me
a hot bubble-bath, stepped in and blew me
through a slit in his rubber suit, threw me

a vast scented mother of all towels,
said 'that was all right' with his rubbery vowels,
delved on pointy rubber feet like trowels

into the kitchen debris, found an egg,
poured coffee like a diver at a keg,
my merman, and he'd neither brag nor beg,

just *was*, the life he led, I thought it weird
but then I thought it not so weird, geared
to a generous camaraderie, not feared

after the first frisson, and at least no part
of exchange floor, wine-bar, Porsche, the art
of greed – he didn't even have to start

a cahootchy factory, a Soho shop would do! –
it must seem unbelieveable to you,
a suit, a nice one but, that I went through

that perfectly normal – to some! – hoop,
rolling about in a bag, looping the loop –
it's true though – God there's a whole troop

come to loll at the bar now, chaps in chaps,
all caps and studs and bulges and tight straps –
let's get closer, hear them creak, perhaps.

The Mass

'Everything has vanished, there remains a mass.'
Will you feel safe if this should come to pass?
Kill all the species and yet keep the class?

Not at a flash, but something dark crept out
over stone by stone, eating. Not at a shout
something stilled the cars on the roundabout

without a crash, they froze, they turned to smoke.
Not with a roar, black fire dropped on the oak,
wrapped the bluebells in an indigo cloak.

Not with a scream, the lasers at the rave
dimmed, the beat grew distant, faint and grave,
the dancers were spent fireflies in a cave.

And soon the sun went out, the seas were gone,
and every being was silently waited on
by a devouring shadow, and if dawn

came up there was no one left to know,
no eye to see the fields, far less to sow,
no seeds even to will themselves to grow.

But somewhere, we are told, there is a mass,
a body deep under the snuffed-out grass
and garages and graves and interstellar gas,

a pulsing squat magnetic incubator
programmed – slow, slow – to be the reinstator.
How long the vanished wait, till late, and later!

Transclusion

I met a wild man far out in the Net.
He called for any help that he could get.
He dreamed he was in universal debt.

He said the lords of Vega, the commissioners
who prowl the scowling Coalsack take no prisoners.
They kill the access code for late petitioners.

Lost in an overload of gamelans,
cancer statistics, shark hunts, royal fans,
bibliographies of bibliographies, scans

for cloning, fractal landscapes, hacker jokes,
monologues from interstellar soaks,
the buzz, the garbage, the mad search, the hoax –

he shivered as he pounded the last key
and got a void, then a high summons, and then me.
I told him, though we suffered, we were free,

there was no debt, rather the universe
was in debt to us, and we could still immerse
its terrors in one tear, one line of verse,

the spring of consciousness it can't unparch,
the love it passes blindly in its march
through darkness to an untriumphal arch.

He wept a little, as I left him there,
but tapped his *adios*. I made him swear
an everlasting rain check on despair.

Day's End

'Adieu paniers, vendanges sont faites!'
The grapes are bustling and the sun has set.
Rich loads go creaking into twilight yet.

The work is done, the harvest songs are sung.
The dripping nets are full, the prey is sprung.
Cloths are scrubbed and rinsed and wrung and hung.

The ship's horn draws its travellers into port.
The starlings wheel across their city fort.
The moon has cycled into the backcourt.

The rave queue melts into the brilliant door.
The stars are ice. Jugs of darkness pour.
The lovers' bedspread slithers to the floor.

The night wind rises, and the rain is bold.
The homeless in their doorways clutch the cold,
still real, still waiting for the tale to be told.

Note: The quotations in the first line of some of the poems in the
'Virtual and Other Realities' sequence are from the following
sources: 'Mare Firmum' (Jack Kerouac), 'In the Kitchen'
(Virginia Woolf), 'More Questions than Answers' (Mina Pater),
'The Poet' (Ezra Pound), 'Early Days' (William Cowper),
'Universes' (Sir Bernard Lovell), 'Indefinables' (Fyodor
Tyutchev), 'Zaum' (Kazimir Malevich), 'Marlowe' (The English
Faust Book), 'Marginalization' (Antonio Gramsci), 'The Mass'
(Kazimir Malevich), 'Day's End' (French saying, 'the business
is completed').

ARIEL FREED

Ariel Freed

I lifted my wings at midnight.
Moonlit pines, empty paths,
broochlike lagoons dwindled below me.
Oh I was electric: my wingtips
winked like stars through the real stars.
Cold, brisk, tingling that journey,
voyage more than journey, the night
had waves, pressures I had to breast,
thrust aside, I had a figurehead or
perhaps I was a figurehead with
dolphins of the darkness as companions.
Only to have no shore, no landfall,
no runway, no eyrie, no goal and no fall!